CAMBRIDGE
UNIVERSITY PRESS

CAMBRIDGE ENGLISH
Language Assessment
Part of the University of Cambridge

CW00701085

Second Edition

Kid's Box
for Ecuador

Student's Book 2A
American English

Caroline Nixon & Michael Tomlinson
Ecuadorian CLIL content by Kate Cory-Wright and Jill Hadfield

Thanks and Acknowledgments

Authors' thanks

Many thanks to everyone at Cambridge University Press and in particular to:

Rosemary Bradley for supervising the whole project and for her keen editorial eye;
Emily Hird for her energy, enthusiasm, and enormous organizational capacity;
Claire Appleyard for all her hard work and sound contributions;
Colin Sage for his good ideas and helpful suggestions;
Karen Elliot for her enthusiasm and creative reworking of the Phonics sections.

We would also like to thank all our pupils and colleagues at Star English, El Palmar, Murcia, and especially Jim Kelly and Julie Woodman for their help and suggestions at various stages of the project.

Dedications

I would like to dedicate this book to the women who have been my pillars of strength: Milagros Marín, Sara de Alba, Elia Navarro, and Maricarmen Balsalobre - CN

To Paloma, for her love, encouragement, and unwavering support. Thanks. - MT

The Authors and Publishers would like to thank the following teachers for their help in reviewing the material and for the invaluable feedback they provided:

Alice Matovich, Cecilia Sanchez, Florencia Durante, Maria Loe Antigona, Argentina; Erica Santos, Brazil; Ma Xin, Ren Xiaochi, China; Albeiro Monsalve Marin, Colombia; Agata Jankiewicz, Poland; Maria Antonia Castro, Spain; Catherine Taylor, Turkey.

The authors and publishers would like to thank the following consultants for their invaluable feedback:

Coralyn Bradshaw, Pippa Mayfield, Hilary Ratcliff, Melanie Williams.

We would also like to thank all the teachers who allowed us to observe their classes and who gave up their invaluable time for interviews and focus groups.

The authors and publishers acknowledge the following sources of copyright material and are grateful for the permissions granted. While every effort has been made, it has not always been possible to identify the sources of all the material used or to trace all copyright holders. If any omissions are brought to our notice, we will be happy to include the appropriate acknowledgments on reprinting.

t = top, c = center, b = below, l = left, r = right

p.16 (orange): Shutterstock/Maks Narodenko; p.16 (banana): Shutterstock/brulove; p.16 (apple): Shutterstock/Roman Samokhin; p.16 (pear): Shutterstock/Andrey Eremin; p.16 (pineapple): Shutterstock/Alex Staroseltsev; p.16 (lemon): Shutterstock/topseller; p.17 (t): Thinkstock; p.31 (t): Thinkstock; p.31 (1): Thinkstock/iStockphoto; p.31 (2): Shutterstock/Sergey Karpov; p.31 (3): Shutterstock/Aron Brand; p.31 (4): Shutterstock/Feng Yu; p.31 (bl): Shutterstock/Picsfive; p.31 (bc): Shutterstock/Skylines; p.31 (br): Shutterstock/Quang Ho; p. 31a (tl, tr, bl): Getty Images/Ryan McVay/Photodisc; p. 31a (br): Getty Images/Digital Zoo/Photodisc; p.32 (11): Shutterstock/Iwona Grodzka; p.32 (12): Shutterstock/K. Miri Photography; p.32 (13): Shutterstock/DenisNata; p.32 (14): Shutterstock/Luis Carlos Torres; p.32 (15): Shutterstock/Masalski Maksim; p.32 (16): Shutterstock/terekhov igor; p.32 (17): Shutterstock/Nikuwka; p.32 (18): Alamy/Graham Morley; p.32 (19): Alamy/Mike Stone; p.32 (20): Shutterstock/Mostphotos; p.46 (tl): Alamy/Christine Whitehead; p.46 (tc): Shutterstock/Paul Cowan; p.46 (tr): Shutterstock/Nattika; p.46 (bl): Shutterstock/Diana Taliun; p.46 (bc): Shutterstock/Nattika; p.46 (br): Shutterstock/Maks Narodenko; p.47 (t): Thinkstock; p.60 (1): Shutterstock/agrosse; p. 47a (cake): Getty Images/Alfonso Acedo/Moment; p. 47a (ice cream, cola): Getty Images/unalozmen/iStock; p. 47a (Lollipop): Getty Images/Noppol Mahawanjam/iStock; p. 47a (juice): Getty Images/Okea/iStock; p. 47a (corn): Getty Images/danleap/E+; p. 47a (yogurt): Getty Images/Dorling Kindersley; p. 47a (meat): Getty Images/Carin Krasner/Photolibrary; p. 47a (french fries): Getty Images/Food Image Source/StockFood Creative; p. 47a (tuna): Getty Images/PhotoEuphoria/iStock; p. 47a (egg): Getty Images/blackred/E+.

Cover photography by Julie Watson.

Background image on pages 17a, 17b, 31a, 31b, 47a, 47b by Getty Images/madebymarco/iStock.

Commissioned photography on pages 7, 8, 14, 17b, 22, 28, 30, 35, 38, 44 by Trevor Clifford Photography.

Commissioned photography on page 31b by Julie Watson.

The authors and publishers are grateful to the following illustrators:

Andrew Hennessey; Beatrice Costamagna, c/o Pickled ink; Bethan Matthews, c/o Syvlie Poggio; c/o Chris Garbutt, c/o Arena; John Batten, c/o Beehive Illustration; Lucía Serrano Guerroro; Kelly Kennedy, c/o Syvlie Poggio; Rob McKlurkan, c/o The Bright Agency; Andrew Painter; Melanie Sharp, c/o Syvlie Poggio; Marie Simpson, c/o Pickled ink; Emily Skinner, c/o Graham-Cameron Illustration; Lisa Smith; Gary Swift; Lisa Williams, c/o Sylvie Poggio;

The publishers are grateful to the following contributors:

Louise Edgeworth: picture research and art direction
Wild Apple Design Ltd: page design
Blooberry: additional design
Melanie Sharp: cover illustration
John Green and Tim Woolf, TEFL Audio: audio recordings
John Marshall Media, Inc. and Lisa Hutchins: audio recordings for the American English edition
Robert Lee: song writing
hyphen S.A.: publishing management, American English edition

Language summary

	Key vocabulary	**Key grammar and functions**	**Phonics**
1 Hi again! page 4	**Character names:** *Mr. Star, Mrs. Star, Sally, Scott, Suzy, Grandma Star, Grandpa Star, Marie, Maskman, Monty, Trevor* **Numbers:** *1–10* **Colors:** *red, yellow, pink, green, orange, blue, purple, brown, black, white, gray*	**Greetings:** *Hi, we're the Star family. Who's he/she? This is my brother, Scott. He's seven, and this is my sister, Suzy. She's four.* **Prepositions:** *in, on, under*	Long vowel sound: "ay" (pl<u>ay</u>)
2 Back to school page 10	**Character names:** *Alex, Robert, Eva* **School:** *bookcase, board, cupboard, computer, desk, ruler, teacher, TV, whiteboard* **Numbers:** *11–20*	*How many (books) are there? There are/aren't (ten desks). Is there (a ruler) on the (desk)? Yes, there is. / No there isn't. Are there (ten pens) on the (desk)? Yes, there are. / No, there aren't.* **Prepositions:** *next to*	Long vowel sound: "ee" (thr<u>ee</u>)

3 Play time! page 18	**Toys:** *alien, camera, computer game, kite, robot, truck, watch*	*this, these Whose (backpack) is this? It's Tom's. Whose (shoes) are these? They're Sue's.*	Long vowel sound: "i" (f<u>i</u>ve, fl<u>y</u>)
4 At home page 24	**Furniture:** *bathtub, bed, clock, couch, lamp, mirror, phone, rug*	*It's mine. It's yours. Is that hat yours? Yes, it is. / No, it isn't. Are those blue socks yours? Yes, they are. / No, they aren't.*	Long vowel sound: "oa/o_e" (b<u>oa</u>t, ph<u>o</u>ne)

5 Meet my family page 34	**Character names:** *Tony, Alice, Nick, Kim, Hugo, Lucy, May, Robert, Sam, Frank* **Family:** *baby, cousin, mom, dad, grandma, grandpa*	*What are you doing? I'm reading. What's Grandpa doing? He's sleeping.* **Verb + -ing spellings:** *hitting, running, sitting, swimming* **Verbs:** *catch, clean, fly, get, hit, jump, kick, run, sit, sleep, talk, throw*	Long vowel sound: "oo" (bl<u>ue</u>, r<u>u</u>ler)
6 Dinner time page 40	**Food:** *bread, chicken, eggs, fries, juice, milk, rice, water*	*Can I have some (egg and fries)? Here you are.*	Consonant sound: "ch" (<u>ch</u>icken)

1 Hi again!

1 CD1 2 Listen and point.

2 CD1 3 Listen and repeat.

4

3 **4** **CD1** 💬 Listen and answer.

Hi, I'm Trevor. Look at number four. Who's he?

4 💬 Ask and answer.

Look at number three. Who's she?

Sally.

Vocabulary

Suzy   Scott   Sally   Mr. Star
Mrs. Star   Grandpa Star   Grandma Star

Grammar

What's your name?   How old are you?
Who's he/she?

🔊 5 CD1 💬 Listen, point, and repeat.

a b c d
e f g
h i j k
l m n o p
q r s
t u v
w x y z

6 🔊 6 CD1 💬 Say the chant.

1

7 Ask and answer.

gray
pink
green
orange
red
brown
white
blue
yellow
black
purple

Can you spell "purple"?

P-u-r-p-l-e.

8 Order the colors.

Black, blue, brown …

snake

play

game

Four snakes are playing games!

10 💬 Say and answer.

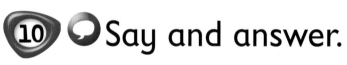

The pencil is under the chair.

That's h.

a

h

j

k

11 **13** CD1 # Listen to the story.

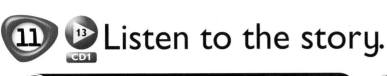

1 a, b, c, d, e, f, g ...

2 Let's play a game. What's this color? B-l-u-e.

I know. It's blue. My car's blue. Look!

3 Now, it's my turn. What's this word? F-o-u-r.

I know. That's four. Here are four pencils! My turn.

4 What's this, Trevor? P-u-r-p-l-e.

Uh. Is it a pencil? Pencils are my favorite food.

No, Trevor. It's purple. Your hair's purple.

5 OK, Trevor. It's your turn.

Uh. What's this? T-h-r-e-e.

Three. I only have three pencils!

6 Where's the red pencil?

Are pencils your favorite food, Trevor?

Uh, yes, they are. Sorry, Monty.

12 **14** CD1 # Listen and say the number.

2 Back to school

1 🔊 16 CD1 Listen and point.

board

cupboard

teacher

bookcase

ruler

desk

2 🔊 17 CD1 Listen and repeat.

3 🔊19 CD1 💬 Listen and point. Chant.

School, school. This is the Numbers School.

11   Eleven desks,
12   Twelve erasers,
13   Thirteen rulers,
14   Fourteen cupboards,
15   Fifteen classrooms,
16   Sixteen teachers,
17   Seventeen pens,
18   Eighteen boards,
19   Nineteen pencils,
20   Twenty tables.

School, school. This is the Numbers School.

$1 \times 3 =$
$2 \times 4 =$

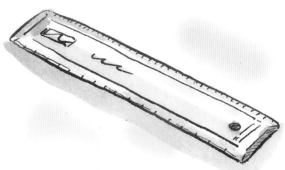

4 💬 Ask and answer.

How many desks are there?   11.

Vocabulary

board   bookcase   cupboard   desk   ruler   teacher

5 🔊 CD1 20 👂 Listen and point.

This is my classroom. How many desks are there? There are a lot of desks. That's my desk next to the bookcase. There's a long pink ruler on it. There are a lot of books in the bookcase. There's a big whiteboard on the wall. There's a computer, but there isn't a TV.

6 🔊 CD1 21 💬 Listen and repeat.

Grammar

How many … are there?   There is …   There are …

7   ♪Listen and point. Sing.

There are pencils in the classroom, yes, there are.
There's a cupboard on the pencils, yes, there is.
There's a ruler on the cupboard,
There's a bookcase on the ruler,
There's a teacher on the bookcase, yes, there is …

8 Ask and answer.

Where's the cupboard?　　On the pencils.

3

three

teacher

tree

Three teachers sleeping in a tree!

10 💬 Say and correct.

> There are three posters in the classroom.

> No, there aren't. There are two posters.

26 CD1 # Listen to the story.

12 **27** CD1 # Listen and say "yes" or "no."

1 🔊28 CD1 **Listen and point.**

| orange | banana | apple | pear | pineapple | lemon |

2 🔊29 CD1 **Listen and answer.**

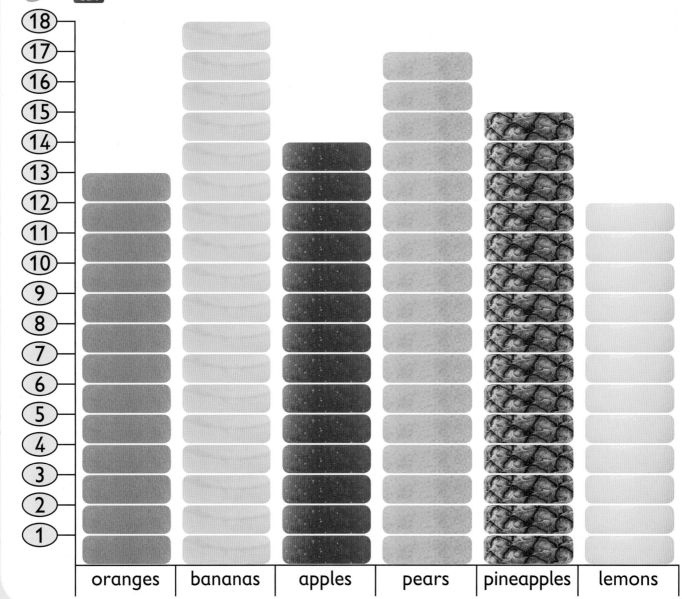

| oranges | bananas | apples | pears | pineapples | lemons |

Vocabulary
lemon   pear   pineapple

Now you!
Workbook page 16

3   Listen and say the number.

4 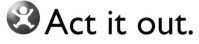 Act it out.

Functions

After you.   Thank you.   Can you … please?   Yes, of course.
Can we come in?   Yes, come in.

1 🎧 ✋ Listen and point.

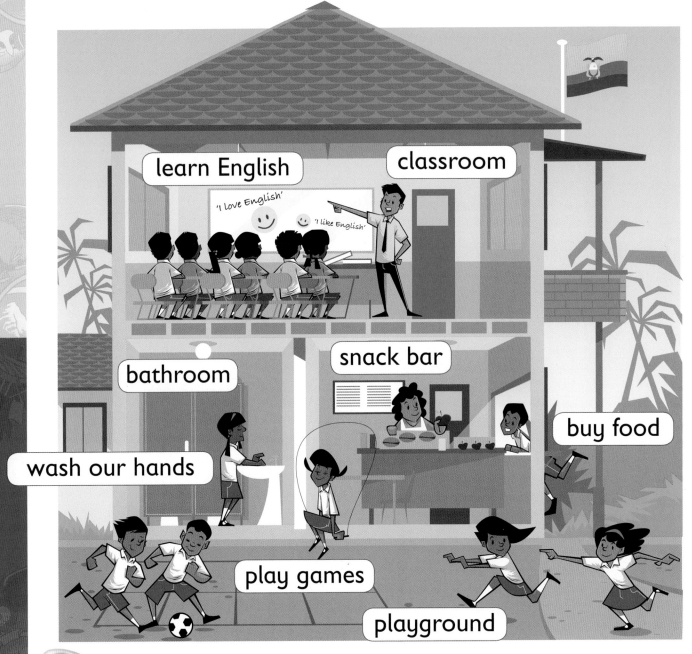

learn English

classroom

'I love English'

'I like English'

bathroom

snack bar

buy food

wash our hands

play games

playground

2 💬 Ask and answer.

Where do we wash our hands?　In the bathroom.

3 🧒💬 Play the game. Ask and guess.

Where am I?

No.

Yes.

Do we wash our hands there?

Do we buy food there?

You're in the snack bar!

Language through the arts

4 🎵✏️ Sing the song.
Write your own verse.

This is where we wash our hands,
wash our hands, wash our hands.
This is where we wash our hands,
In the bathroom, bathroom, bathroom.

This is where we buy our food, buy our food,
buy our food.
This is where we buy our food,
In the snack bar, snack bar, snack bar.

This is where ...

3 Play time!

1 🔊31 CD1 Listen and point.

Toys 4 U

Kites

kite

Trucks

Watches

Cameras

watch

camera

Computer games

truck

Robots

Metal mouth

alien

robot

computer game

2 🔊32 CD1 Listen and repeat.

18

3 🔊 34 CD1 💬 Listen and say the number.

These are dolls. 19. This is a robot. 17.

4 🔊 35 CD1 💬 Listen and say "yes" or "no."

Vocabulary: alien camera computer game kite robot truck watch

Grammar: this these

5 Listen and point.

  6 Listen and repeat.

Grammar

Whose is this?   Whose are these?

Listen and point. Sing.

Whose jacket is this? ...
What? That black jacket?
Yes, this black jacket.
Whose jacket is this?
It's John's.
Oh!

Whose shoes are these? ...
What? Those blue shoes?
Yes, these blue shoes.
Whose shoes are these?
They're Sheila's.
Oh!

Whose skirt is this? ...
What? That purple skirt?
Yes, this purple skirt.
Whose skirt is this?
It's Sue's.
Oh!

Whose pants are these? ...
What? Those brown pants?
Yes, these brown pants.
Whose pants are these?
They're Tom's.
Oh!

8 **Ask and answer.**

Whose pants are these?   They're Tom's.

Monty's phonics

9 · 41 · CD1

fly

5 five

kite

I'm flying my five white kites.

10 Ask and answer.

11. Whose nose is this?

It's Scott's.

12. Whose eyes are these?

They're Sally's.

11 12 13 14 15 16 17 18

11 🎧 44 CD1 Listen to the story.

1
Whose robot is this?

It's Scott's.

2
Hi. What's your name?

My name is Metal Mouth.

3
Oh. Can you walk, Metal Mouth?

I can walk, and I can talk.

4
Well, I can walk. I can talk, and I can spell. U-g-l-y.

5
I know! I know! It's ugly!

Yes, it is … and it can't fly.

6
Maskman! Say "sorry," please.

Sorry.

It's OK, Maskman. You're a superhero, and you're Scott's favorite toy.

12 ❌ Act out the story.

4 At home

1 🎵46 CD1 👀 Listen and point.

mirror

rug

couch

clock

phone

lamp

2 🎵47 CD1 💬 Listen and repeat.

24

3 CD1 49 💬 Listen and point. Chant.

There's a mirror in the bathroom,
And a phone in the hallway.
A couch in the living room,
A clock on the wall.
There's a lamp on the table,
And a rug next to the bed.
There's a boat in the bathtub,
And the boat is red.

4 CD1 50 💬 Listen and correct.

There's a boy sitting on the couch.

Vocabulary

clock   couch   lamp   mirror   phone   rug

6 Listen and repeat.

Grammar

It's mine/yours.

7   Listen and point. Sing.

Look at this!
Look at this!

Whose shoes are these? ...
Sally! Are they yours? ...
No, they aren't mine! ...

Hmm. Which shoes are Scott's? ...
Which, which, which, which?
Which shoes are Scott's?
The gray ones are his ...

Hmm. Which shoes are Suzy's? ...
Which, which, which, which?
Which shoes are Suzy's?
The red ones are hers ...

SO! Whose shoes are those? ...
Whose, whose, whose, whose?
Whose shoes are those?
Those are Grandpa's ...
Grandpa's?

GRANDPA!

8 Ask and answer.

Which backpack is yours?   The red one's mine.

9 🔊 57 💬 Monty's phonics

CD1

phone

yellow

boat

A phone in a yellow boat!

10 🔍💬 Find your partner.

Are these pants yours or mine?

They're mine.

28

11 Listen to the story.

12 Listen and say the number.

Marie's art — Origami

1 CD2 🔊 Listen and say.

What is it?   It's a kite.

2 🔍💬 What do you think this is?

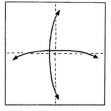 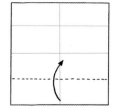 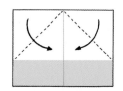 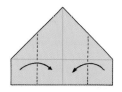

Now you!
Workbook page 30

3 ▶ CD2 💬 Listen and say the number.

1

2

3

4

4 🔍 💬 Ask and answer.

(What's this?)　(It's a flowerpot.)　(What's it made from?)　(It's made from a boot.)

5 💬 What do you reuse at home?

(I reuse ... at home.)

(bottles)　(paper)　(plastic bags)

1 👂💬 Listen, point, and say.

1 a blindfold

2 hit / a stick

3 break

4 candy

2 💬 Ask and answer.

What can you see in number 1?

He's breaking the piñata.

No, he has a blindfold and a stick.

He's breaking the piñata.

He has a blindfold and a stick.

There's a lot of candy.

He's hitting the piñata.

3 💬 Talk about the pictures.

| piñata   color   toy |

Do you like this …?

What's your favorite …?

Language through the arts

4 ✏️ Design a piñata, a stick, and a blindfold.

My piñata is a blue boat. It has …

Review

1 🔊💬 Listen and say the number.

11 **12** **13** **14** **15**

16 **17** **18** **19** **20**

2 🔍💬 Look and say.

> In picture one, there's a purple mat on the floor, but in picture two there's a purple rug on the floor.

1

2

3 Play the game. Ask and answer.

What's this?   A cupboard.

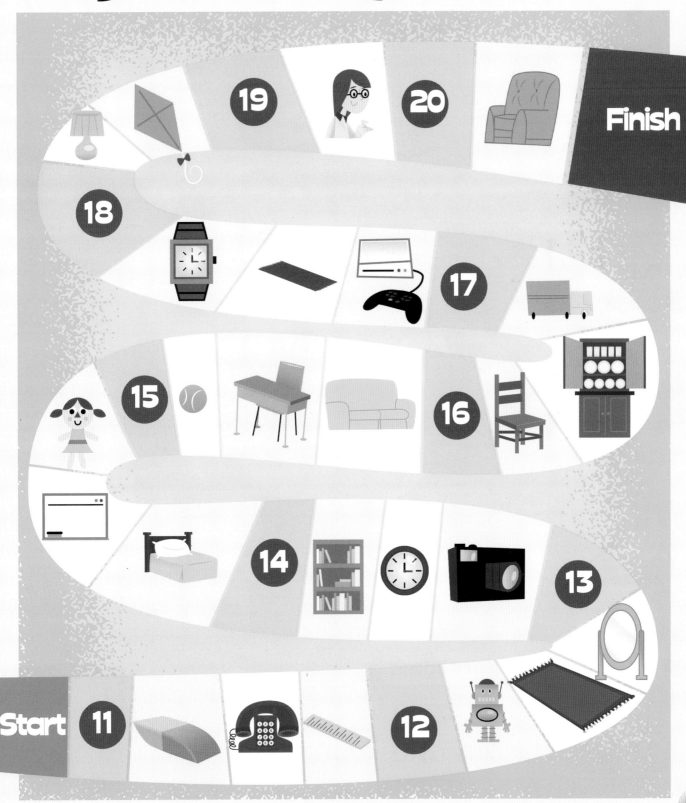

5 Meet my family

1 CD2 Listen and point.

Park

mom

dad

cousin

baby

grandpa

grandma

2 CD2 Listen and repeat.

34

3   Listen and answer.

Tony   Alice

Nick   Kim   Hugo   Lucy

May   Robert   Sam   Frank

4 Look and say.

He's Robert's father.

Nick.

She's Hugo's mother.

Alice.

Vocabulary

baby   cousin   mom   dad   grandma   grandpa

35

5 [9 CD2] Listen and say the number.

6 Make sentences. Use the words in the box.

The dog's getting the ball.

| getting | throwing | catching | flying | talking | jumping |
| sitting | hitting | cleaning | running | kicking | sleeping |

Grammar
He's/She's ...ing

Vocabulary
catch   clean   fly   get   hit   jump   run   sleep   throw

7  **Listen and point. Sing.**

My grandpa isn't walking,
He's flying my favorite kite.
My grandma's cleaning the table,
It's beautiful and white.
My father's playing baseball,
He can catch, and he can hit.
My cousin has the ball now,
And now he's throwing it.

My baby sister's sleeping,
She is very small.
My brother isn't jumping,
He's kicking his soccer ball.
Hey!

My grandpa isn't walking,
He's flying my favorite kite.
My grandma's cleaning the table,
It's beautiful and white.
My mother's sitting reading,
Her book is big and gray.
And me? I'm very happy,
I can run and play ...

8 **Ask and answer.**

(What's Grandpa doing?)   (He's flying a kite.)

blue

ruler

Sue

Sue has a big blue ruler!

10 💬 **Ask and answer.**

What's Scott doing?

He's sleeping

11 **16** **Listen to the story.**

1. Ooh! What's he doing to those shoes, Marie?

   He's cleaning them, Trevor.

2. Hi, Trevor! Look at me! I'm driving Suzy's yellow truck.

3. Hi, Maskman. What are you doing?

   I'm flying my helicopter. I'm a superhero.

4. Hi, Marie. What are you doing?

   I'm cleaning my shoes.

5. What are you doing, Trevor?

   I'm cleaning the dollhouse.

6. Oh, no!

12 **17** **Listen and say the number.**

6 Dinner time

1 19 CD2 Listen and point.

bread
rice
milk
juice
water
eggs
fries
chicken

2 20 CD2 Listen and repeat.

3 🎵 Listen and point. Sing.

It's morning, it's morning.
We're having breakfast with our mom.
Bread and milk, bread and milk.
It's morning, it's morning.

It's lunchtime, it's lunchtime.
We're having lunch with our friends.
Eggs and fries, eggs and fries.
It's lunchtime, it's lunchtime.

It's afternoon, it's afternoon.
We're having a snack in the backyard.
Chocolate cake, chocolate cake.
We're having a snack in the afternoon.

It's evening, it's evening.
We're having dinner with Mom and Dad.
Chicken and rice, chicken and rice.
It's evening, it's evening ...

4 Point, ask, and answer.

What's this?   It's chocolate cake.   What are these?   They're fries.

Vocabulary
bread   chicken   eggs   fries   juice   milk   rice   water

6 🔊 24 CD2 💬 Listen and repeat.

Grammar

Can I have some … ? Here you are.

7 👥 Play bingo.

8 🔍💬 Read and answer.

Hi. My name's Alex. I'm Scott's friend. It's lunchtime, and I'm having and 🍟 for lunch. isn't my favorite lunch. My favorite lunch is ⚫.

In the morning my favorite breakfast is 🍎 and , and my favorite dinner is and 🥣.

1 What's his favorite breakfast?

2 What's his favorite lunch?

3 What's his favorite dinner?

Monty's phonics

chicken

kitchen

The **ch**ickens are cooking in the ki**tch**en!

10 Ask and answer.

Can I have some bread, please?

Here you are.

11 🔘 Listen to the story.

12 🔘 Listen and say "yes" or "no."

1  Look and say.

Where is milk from?

Animals.

animals

trees

plants

2 30 CD2 Listen and correct.

Eggs are from trees.

No, eggs are from animals.

Vocabulary

meat   plant   tree

Now you!
Workbook page 46

3 🎧31 CD2 💬 Listen and say the number.

Breakfast

1

2

Lunch

3

4

Dinner

5

6

4 💬 Ask and answer.

What's number one?

It's a bad breakfast.

What's number four?

It's a good lunch.

1 **Listen and point.**

a lot

some

a little bit

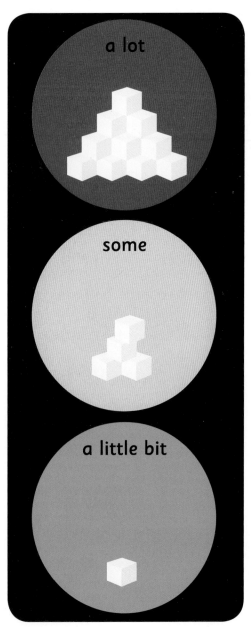

soda

candy

yogurt

corn

2 **Ask and answer.**

Ice cream?

A lot.

3 🔍 Read, look, and match.

1 There's a lot of sugar in soda.

2 There's a little bit of sugar in bread.

3 There's some sugar in yogurt.

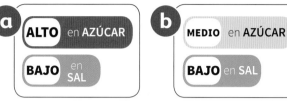

a
ALTO en AZÚCAR
BAJO en SAL

b
MEDIO en AZÚCAR
BAJO en SAL

c
BAJO en AZÚCAR
BAJO en SAL

Language through the arts

4 ✏️ Draw three plates. Draw food.

BAJO en AZÚCAR

MEDIO en AZÚCAR

ALTO en AZÚCAR

5 ✏️ 🎵 Write and sing.

GREEN AND **YELLOW**

Let's eat some chicken now,
Let's drink some water, too.
Meat, corn, eggs, fish,
Are very good for me!

RED

Let's eat some .... cake,
Let's drink some .... ,too.
Ice cream, ...
Are very .... for me!

You eat a little bit of sugar,
Then you stop! Go out and play!
That's what it's all about.

Vocabulary
a little bit   candy   corn   soda   sugar   yogurt

Grammar reference

1

Who's he?	This is my brother, Scott. He's seven.
Who's she?	This is my sister, Suzy. She's four.

Who's he? = Who is he?   he's = he is   she's = she is

2

How many **desks** are there?	There are **a lot of desks**.
Is there **a whiteboard** on **the wall**?	Yes, there is. / No, there isn't.
Are there **ten desks** in **the classroom**?	Yes, there are. / No, there aren't.

there's = there is   there aren't = there are not

3

Whose **camera** is **this**?	It's Scott's.
Whose **books** are **these**?	They're Suzy's.

It's Scott's. = It's Scott's camera.
They're Suzy's. = They're Suzy's books.

4

Whose **green T-shirt** is that?	It's mine.
Whose **socks** are those?	They're yours.
Is that dress yours, Suzy?	Yes, it is. / No, it isn't.
Are those **socks** yours, Scott?	Yes, they are. / No, they aren't.

It's mine. = It's my T-shirt.   No, they aren't. = No, they are not.

5

I'm	sing**ing**.
He's/She's	not **fly**ing.
You're/They're/We're	
What are you doing, Suzy?	
What's Grandpa do**ing**?	

6

Can I have **some chicken**, please?	Here you are.

Kid's Box for Ecuador

American English

Workbook 2A

Caroline Nixon & Michael Tomlinson

Hi again!

1  Write.

I'm Sally. I'm Scott. I'm Suzy.

She's *Sally.* He's _____ _____

I'm Mr. Star. I'm Mrs. Star. I'm Grandpa.

Hi, I'm Grandma Star. This is my family.

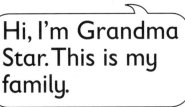   

_____ _____ _____

2 Draw and write.

What's your name? **Me!**

_____

How old are you?

_____

3  Color the stars.

1 ★ ★ ☆ ☆ ☆ ☆ ☆ ☆ ☆ ☆
Color two stars.

2 ☆ ☆ ☆ ☆ ☆ ☆ ☆ ☆ ☆ ☆
Color five stars.

3 ☆ ☆ ☆ ☆ ☆ ☆ ☆ ☆ ☆ ☆
Color six stars.

4 ☆ ☆ ☆ ☆ ☆ ☆ ☆ ☆ ☆ ☆
Color one star.

5 ☆ ☆ ☆ ☆ ☆ ☆ ☆ ☆ ☆ ☆
Color eight stars.

4  Match and connect.

1 four + one =   7   eight

2 two + one =   5   seven

3 six + one =   8   five

4 eight + one =   6   ten

5 five + one =   9   six

6 seven + one =   10   three

7 nine + one =   3   nine

5 🔊 7 CD1 ✏️ Listen and color.

t e b c d g p v

6 🔊 8 CD1 ✏️ Listen and point. Write the words.

lylaS   Szuy   ctoSt   frou   igteh   sneev

1 This is __Sally.__
She's __eight.__

2 This is _____
He's _____

3 This is _____
She's _____

7 Read the question. Listen and write a name or a number. There are two examples.

Example

What is the boy's name? .....*Dan*.....

How old is he? .....*9*.....

Questions

(1) What is the girl's name? ....

(2) How old is the girl? ....

(3) What is the name of Dan's street? ....
Street

(4) What number is Dan's house? ....

(5) What is the name of Grace's book? ....
House

8 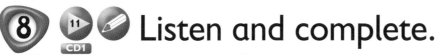 **Listen and complete.**

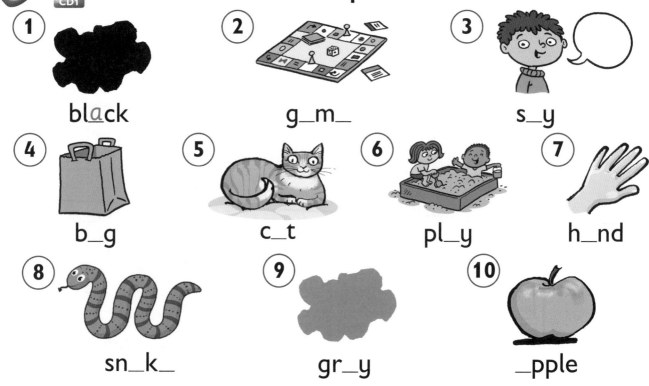

1. black
2. g_m_
3. s_y
4. b_g
5. c_t
6. pl_y
7. h_nd
8. sn_k_
9. gr_y
10. _pple

9 **Listen and write. Match.**

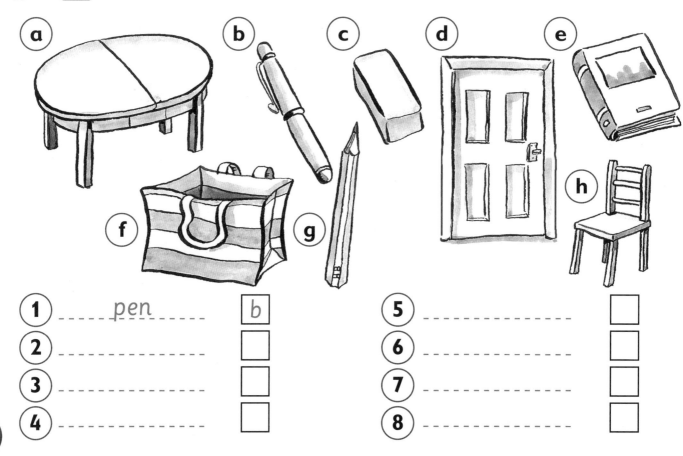

a b c d e

f g h

1. _pen_ | b |
2. ___ | |
3. ___ | |
4. ___ | |
5. ___ | |
6. ___ | |
7. ___ | |
8. ___ | |

My picture dictionary

10 Listen and write. Stick.

① _purple_

② _____

③ _____

④ _____

⑤ _____

⑥ _____

My progress

Check (✓) or put an ✗.

I can count to ten. ☐

I can say the colors. ☐

I can say the alphabet. ☐

1  Find and write the words.

desk

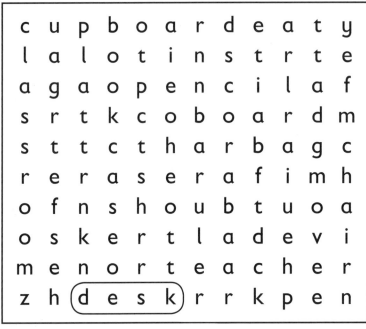

```
c u p b o a r d e a t y
l a l o t i n s t r t e
a g a o p e n c i l a f
s r t k c o b o a r d m
s t t c t h a r b a g c
r e r a s e r a f i m h
o f n s h o u b t u o a
o s k e r t l a d e v i
m e n o r t e a c h e r
z h (d e s k) r r k p e n
```

2   Listen and color.

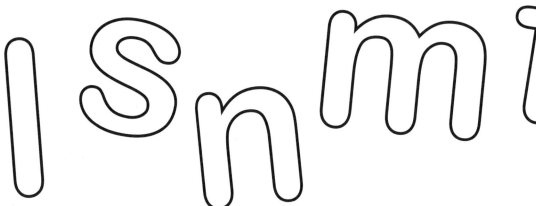

3  Look at the numbers. Write the words.

veleen
11

eleven

niffeet
15

_____

hiegeetn
18

_____

ewletv
12

_____

wytent
20

_____

reihtnet
13

_____

4  Read and color.

(17)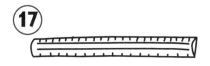

(19)

Color number twelve brown.
Color number nineteen pink.
Color number fourteen green.
Color number seventeen blue.
Color number sixteen orange.

(16)

(14)

(12)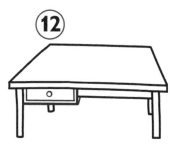

5 ✏️ **Write the sentences.**

① (a ruler) (There's) (the table.) (on)
  There's a ruler on the table.

② (the desk.) (There are) (on) (12 pencils)
  ----

③ (There's) (under) (the chair.) (a backpack)
  ----

④ (the bookcase.) (16 books) (in) (There are)
  ----

6 🔍✏️ **Look at the picture. Write the answer**

① How many burgers are there? *There are six.* _____

② How many apples are there? _____

③ How many oranges are there? _____

④ How many cupcakes are there? _____

⑤ How many ice-cream cones are there? _____

⑥ How many bananas are there? _____

7  Look and read. Write "yes" or "no."

Examples

There are two teachers in the classroom. _no_

There's a poster on the wall. _yes_

Questions

(1) There is a door next to the cupboard. _____
(2) There is a board on the wall. _____
(3) There are two tables under the board. _____
(4) There is a ruler on a bookcase. _____
(5) There are three cars under the desk. _____

8 🎧 25 CD1 ✏️ Listen and color red or green.

1. red
2. green
3. tree
4. ten
5. pen
6. read
7. twelve
8. fourteen
9. teacher
10. desk

9 🔍 ✏️ Find the words.

buschoolegrayellowhiteraserulteredesk

How many colors are there? _____

What are they? _____

14

My picture dictionary

  Write the words. Stick.

taechre	baodr	rlure
teacher	_ _ _ _ _	_ _ _ _ _

skde	bkoocsae	cpubaord
_ _ _ _ _	_ _ _ _ _	_ _ _ _ _

My progress

Check (✓) or put an ✗.

I can talk about my classroom. ☐

I can say the numbers 11–20. ☐

I can spell. ☐

Now you! **1**  Ask and answer. Color the graph.

Which animals do you like?

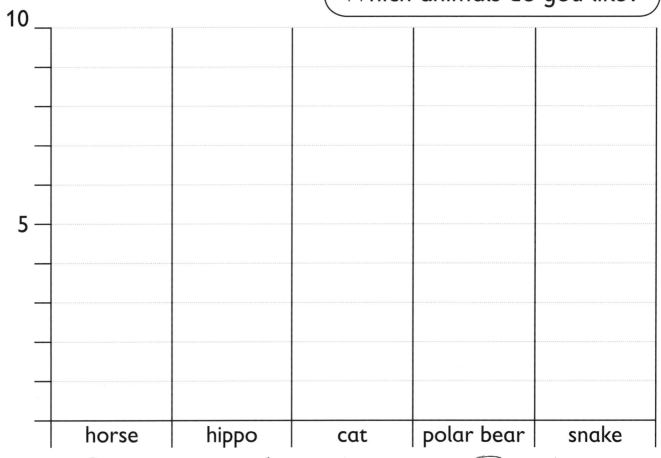

10

5

| horse | hippo | cat | polar bear | snake |

2 Answer the questions.

1 How many children like horses? _ _ _ _ _ _ _ _ _ _

2 How many children like hippos? _ _ _ _ _ _ _ _ _ _

3 How many children like cats? _ _ _ _ _ _ _ _ _ _

4 How many children like polar bears? _ _ _ _ _ _ _ _ _ _

5 How many children like snakes? _ _ _ _ _ _ _ _ _ _

3 Read and complete.

| come in Yes, of course. After you. Can you spell |

 1

 2

– Can we ___come in___, please?
– Yes, come in.

– _____
– Thank you.

 3

 4

– _____
ruler, please?
– Yes, r-u-l-e-r.

– Can you open the window, please?
– _____

4 Draw a picture of you. Be polite!

 Me!

3 Play time!

1 🔍 ✏️ **Read. Circle the "toy" words. Write.**

k i t e

_____ _____

_____

Suzy has a (kite). Scott has a robot. Robert has a train. Eva has a car. Sally has a computer game. Alex has a big yellow watch.

_____ _____

2 🔊33 CD1 ✏️ **Listen and check (✓) the box.**

18

3 ✏️ Complete the sentences and color the pictures.

(1) __This__ is a red plane.

(2) __These__ are purple watches.

(3) _____ are blue trucks.

(4) _____ is a brown doll.

(5) _____ are green tablets.

(6) _____ are gray robots.

(7) _____ are yellow cameras.

(8) _____ are blue kites.

4 ✏️ Match. Write the words.

k	_kitchen_	_kite_	~~itchen~~	obot
c	_____	_____	amera	ain
r	_____	_____	uler	~~ite~~
d	_____	_____	oll	ane
tr	_____	_____	uck	og
pl	_____	_____	ease	ake

5 🔊38 CD1 ✏️ Listen and color. Then answer.

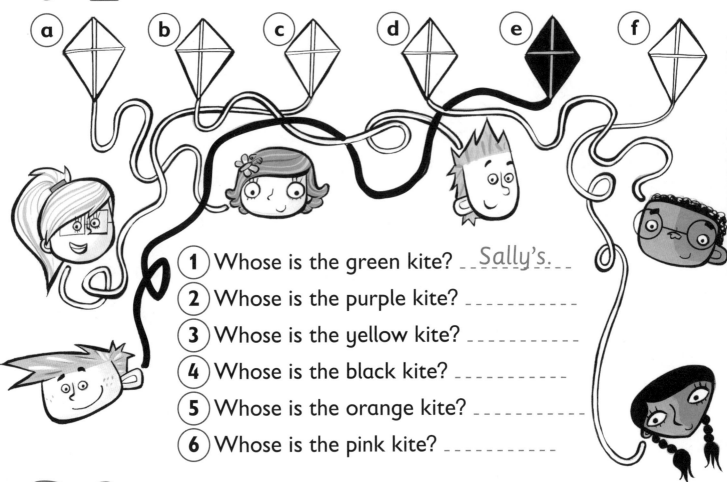

a   b   c   d   e   f

1. Whose is the green kite? _Sally's._
2. Whose is the purple kite? _____
3. Whose is the yellow kite? _____
4. Whose is the black kite? _____
5. Whose is the orange kite? _____
6. Whose is the pink kite? _____

6 ✏️ Write the questions.

1. _Whose is the truck?_ _____ It's Bill's.
2. _____ It's Lucy's.
3. _____ It's Ben's.
4. _____ It's Kim's.
5. _____ It's Tony's.

7 🔍✏️ Look and read. Put a ✓ or an ✗ in the box. There is one example.

Examples

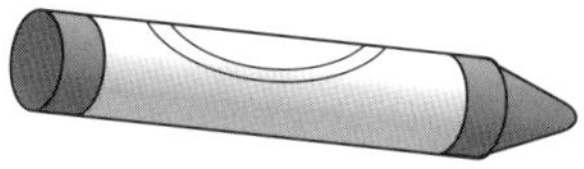

This is a ruler. ☒

These are watches. ☑

Questions

①  These are tablets. ☐

② 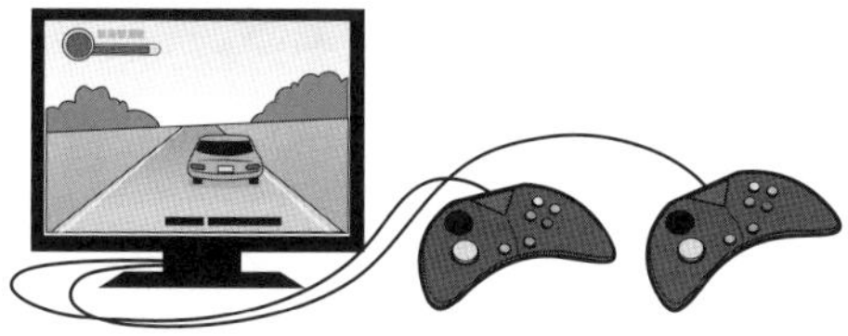 This is a kite. ☐

③  This is a truck. ☐

④  These are trains. ☐

⑤  This is a robot. ☐

8 **42** CD1 **✎** Listen and write the words.

1 ~~fish~~   2 ~~kite~~   3 pink   4 five   5 my

6 swim   7 bike   8 big   9 fly   10 sit

fish

kite

9 **43** CD1 **✎** Listen and connect the dots.

14

6

3

5

2

17

19

1

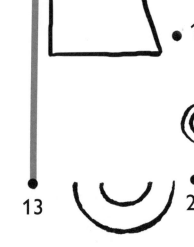

10

8

11

13

20

What is it?   It's a _____ .

My picture dictionary

   Listen and stick. Write the words.

① _ kite _	② _ _ _ _	③ _ _ _ _
④ _ _ _ _	⑤ _ _ _ _	⑥ _ _ _ _

My progress

Check (✓) or put an ✗.

I can talk about my favorite toy. ☐

I can write "toy" words. ☐

4 At home

1 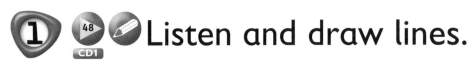 Listen and draw lines.

Bill   Dan   Alice   Eva

Matt   Pat   Lucy

2 Write the words.

	³ m	a	t			
		⁶				
			⁴			
		¹				
		⁷	²		⁸	
⁴						
	⁵					

1	2	3	4	5	6	7	8

3 🔍✏️ Read and write the number. Draw.

sixteen	= _16_ → m	twelve	= _ _ _ _ _ _ → c
fourteen	= _ _ _ _ _ _ → l	fifteen	= _ _ _ _ _ _ → a
seventeen	= _ _ _ _ _ _ → r	thirteen	= _ _ _ _ _ _ → i
eighteen	= _ _ _ _ _ _ → o	nineteen	= _ _ _ _ _ _ → u
twenty	= _ _ _ _ _ _ → p	eleven	= _ _ _ _ _ _ → h

①

m					
16	13	17	17	18	17

②

14	15	16	20

③

12	18	19	12	11

Me!

4 🔍✏️ Read and write the words.

mirror	~~bedroom~~	mat	face	bath

My bathroom is next to my (1) _bedroom_. In my bathroom, I

sit in the (2) _ _ _ _ _ _ _ and wash my body. On the wall, there

is a (3) _ _ _ _ _ _ _ . You can see your (4) _ _ _ _ _ _ _ in it.

There is a blue (5) _ _ _ _ _ _ _ on the floor. You can stand on it.

5 ✏️ Write "yours" or "mine."

1. Whose is this?
   It's _mine_.

2. Is this _ _ _ _ _ _ _ or Scott's?
   It's mine.

3. Is this _ _ _ _ _ _ _ ?
   Yes, it is.

4. Whose are these?
   They're _ _ _ _ _ _ _ .

6 🔊 53 CD1 ✏️ Listen and color.

26

56 Listen and draw lines. There is one example.

Mark   Sue   Kim   Grace

Nick   Hugo   Matt

8 🔊58 CD1 ✏️ Listen and write the words.

(1) ~~boat~~   (2) ~~box~~   (3) doll   (4) phone   (5) clock

(6) clothes   (7) yell<u>ow</u>   (8) ro<u>b</u>ot   (9) socks   (10) old

box

boat

9 ✏️ Write the words.

This   ~~That~~   These   Those   These   That

(1) That is a couch.   (2) _____ is a phone.   (3) _____ are armchairs.

(4) _____ is a clock.   (5) _____ are rugs.   (6) _____ are beds.

My picture dictionary

10 🔍✏️ Complete the words. Stick.

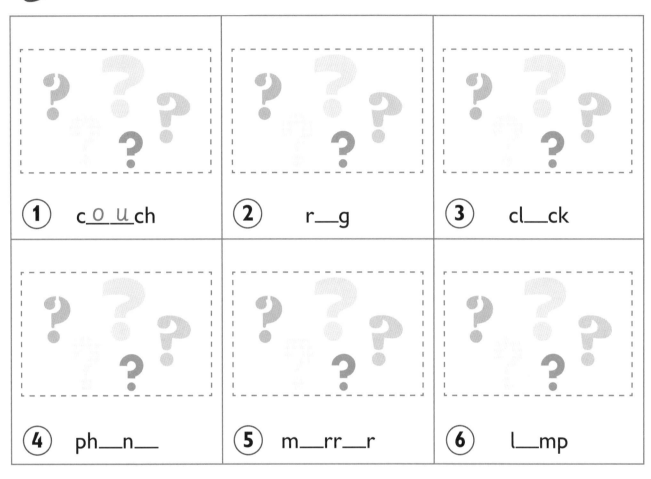

① c_o_u_ch

② r__g

③ cl__ck

④ ph__n__

⑤ m__rr__r

⑥ l__mp

My progress

Check (✓) or put an X.

I can talk about my house. ☐

I can say what's mine. ☐

1 🔍 👤 Make a jumping frog.

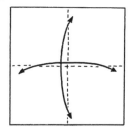 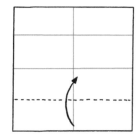 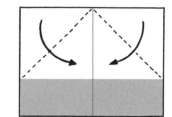 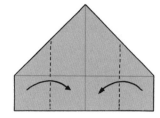

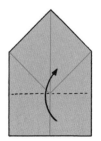 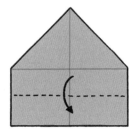 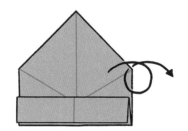 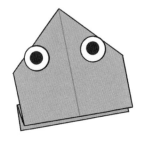

2 🔍 ✏️ Look and write.

~~robot~~ couch cupboard kite phone lamp

①

robot

②

③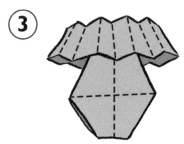

④

⑤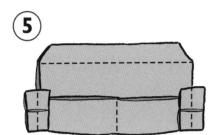

⑥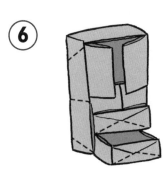

3 🔍 ✏️ Look, read, and match.

①  ② ③ ④

ⓐ an old
 T-shirt

ⓑ an old
 sock

ⓒ old paper

ⓓ a plastic
 bottle

4 ✏️ You have four boxes, two socks, a
 T-shirt, and five pencils. Draw a robot.

Review

1 2 3 4

1 ✏️ Match the color.

7 gray	nine	**8** yellow	three	**5** pink
6 blue	ten	two	**10** orange	four
five	**3** purple	**9** green	eight	**1** brown
2 red	seven	six	**4** black	one

2 🔊 5 CD2 ✏️ Listen and write the number.

13

3 Write the questions. Answer the questions.

	a	b	c	d	e	f
1	what	trucks	dirty	how	big	bed
2	shoes	toy	clean	small	balls	whose
3	is	small	camera	many	are	chair
4	there	under	where	on	the	or

1 4c 3e 4e 1b
Where are the trucks _____ ?
_____ .

2 2f 2b 3a 4d 4e 1f
_____ ?
_____ .

3 3e 4e 2a 2c 4f 1c
_____ ?
_____ .

4 1d 3d 1b 3e 4a
_____ ?
_____ .

5 4c 3a 4e 3c
_____ ?
_____ .

6 1a 3a 4d 4e 3f
_____ ?
_____ .

5 Meet my family

1 🔍✏️ Read and write the names.

This is Robert and his family. He's with his brother Sam, his sister May, and his cousin Frank. Robert's brother has a big nose. Robert has small eyes. Robert's cousin is young. He's a baby. Robert's sister has long hair.

2 ✏️ Write the words.

~~couch~~   ~~mom~~   ~~plane~~   ~~bookcase~~   teacher   grandma   baby
kite   desk   truck   grandpa   playground   cousin   rug   robot
board   mirror   boat   lamp   dad   bed   ruler   doll   phone

In the house
couch

Family
mom

Toys
plane

In the school
bookcase

5

3  Read. Write the name. Color.

Hi. This is my family. My mommy has long purple hair, small green ears, and five yellow teeth. Her name's Trudy. My daddy's name's Tom. He has short red hair and a dirty green nose. He has eight brown teeth. My brother Tony has long brown hair, big red eyes, and one white tooth. My sister's name is Tricia. She's very clean! She has big ears, short blue hair, orange eyes, and six green teeth.

4  Write the words.

bbya   afntharedrg   anthmoredrg   oremth

sstire   fthrea   dda   csinou   rthbore   mmo

baby

baby

5 🔊 ✏️ Listen and write the number.

6 🔍 ✏️ Look at the pictures and write the letters.

1 – What are you doing, Mom?

    – I'm making a cake.

2 – Whose kite are you flying, Scott?

    – I'm flying your kite, Suzy.

3 – What are you eating, Dad?

    – I'm eating chocolate ice cream.

4 – Whose shoes are you cleaning, Grandpa?

    – I'm cleaning Scott's shoes.

5 – Which word are you spelling, Sally?

    – I'm spelling "beautiful."

6 – What are you drawing, Grandma?

    – I'm drawing Sally.

c
d

36

7 **Listen and check (✓) the box.**
There is one example.

Example

What is Dan doing?

Questions

1 Which girl is Anna?

2 What's Sue doing?

3 What's Grandpa doing?

4 What's Sam drawing?

8 🔊15 CD2 ✏️ **Listen and write.**

1. b<u>u</u>s

2. sh___

3. tr_ck

4. S___

5. s_n

6. r_ler

7. bl___

8. r_n

9. j_mp

9 ✏️ **Write the letters.**

a	He's kicking	his car. ☐
b	They're cleaning	in her bed. ☐
c	He's driving	a ball. *a*
d	She's sleeping	books. ☐
e	We're singing	a song. ☐
f	I'm playing	the guitar. ☐
g	They're reading	their rooms. ☐

Listen and write. Stick.

① _grandma_

② _____

③ _____

④ _____

⑤ _____

⑥ _____

 # My progress

Check (✓) or put an ✗.

I can talk about my family. ☐

I can talk about actions. ☐

1 🔍 ✏️ Read the lists and find the food.

Draw lines with a pencil. Draw lines with a pen.

a <u>Shopping list</u>

oranges
bread
rice
bananas
apples
milk
ice cream
burgers
apple juice
eggs
water

b <u>Shopping list</u>

potatoes
rice
bread
carrots
fish
orange juice
fries
chicken
lemons
meat

Start

Start

Finish

Finish

2 🔍 ✏️ **Find and color.**

Color the pears green.
Color the carrots orange.
Color the tomatoes red.

Color the chicken brown.
Color the meat red.
Color the lemons yellow.

3 ✏️💬 **Draw and write about your favorite food. Ask and answer.**

Me!

What's your favorite food for dinner?

It's chicken and fries.

My favorite food is

4 🔊25 CD2 ✏️ Listen and check (✓) or put an **X**.

① **X**

②

③

④

5 🔍 ✏️ **Read and write the numbers.**

Here you are. ☐

Can I have some juice, please? 1

Orange juice, please. ☐

Which juice – orange juice or apple juice? ☐

Which fruit – a banana, a pear, or an apple? ☐

Here you are. ☐

Can I have some fruit, please? ☐

A pear, please. ☐

42

6 🔍✏️ Read and choose a word from the box. Write the word next to numbers 1–5. There is one example.

My breakfast

I eat my breakfast in the _kitchen_ . I sit on a (1) _____ at the table. My dad and my (2) _____ sit with me. My favorite drink for breakfast is (3) _____ , and I eat an (4) _____ with lots of bread. I don't like fruit. My dad loves fruit, and he has two (5) _____ every morning for his breakfast.

Example

~~kitchen~~   egg   bananas   lunch

mirrors   chair   milk   brother

7 Listen and write the words.

teacher   chair   watch   ~~children~~   chicken   kitchen   lunch   chocolate

(1) *children*

(2) _____

(3) _____

(4) _____

(5) _____

(6) _____

(7) _____

(8) _____

8 Write the words and the letters.

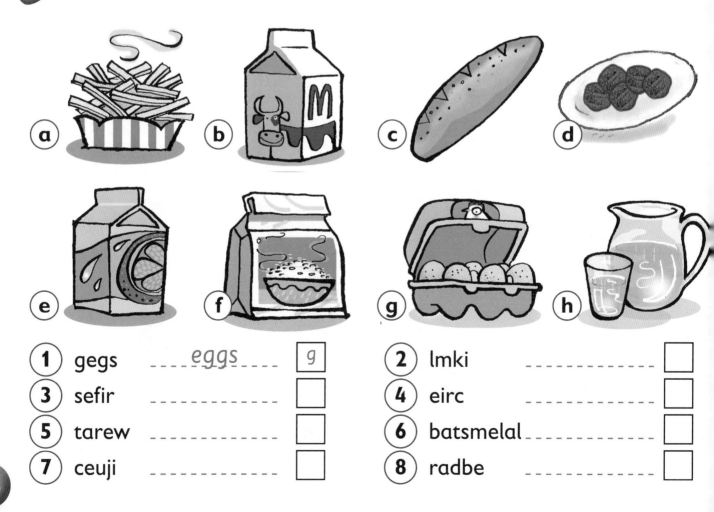

(a)   (b)   (c)   (d)

(e)   (f)   (g)   (h)

(1) gegs   *eggs*   [g]
(2) lmki   _____ [ ]
(3) sefir   _____ [ ]
(4) eirc   _____ [ ]
(5) tarew   _____ [ ]
(6) batsmelal   _____ [ ]
(7) ceuji   _____ [ ]
(8) radbe   _____ [ ]

My picture dictionary

9 Write the words. Stick.

ckinehc	gegs	rifes
chicken		
lkmi	rcie	dearb

My progress

Check (✓) or put an X.

I can talk about my favorite food. ☐

I can talk about breakfast, lunch, ☐ and dinner.

I can ask and answer questions ☐ about food.

1 Read and match.

| milk | meatballs | eggs | lemons | potatoes | carrots |

Now you! 2 Write the words.

| apples   potatoes   milk   carrots   eggs   lemons |
| meat   chicken   oranges   rice   pears   tomatoes |

From animals …   From plants …   From trees …

46

3 Draw your favorite food.

milk   bread   eggs   juice   chicken   rice   water   fish
carrots   apples   meatballs   potatoes   bananas   oranges

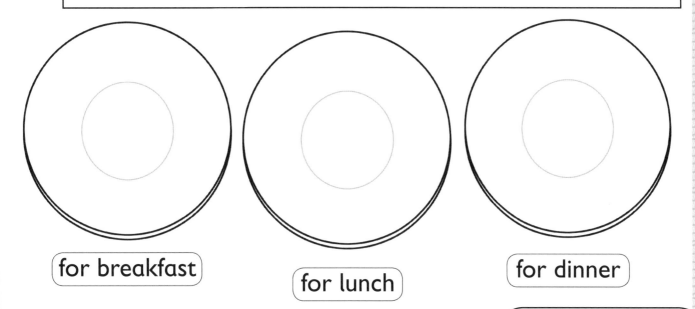

for breakfast

for lunch

for dinner

4 Now tell your partner.
Draw your friend's food.

What's your favorite food for breakfast?

I like oranges and apples.

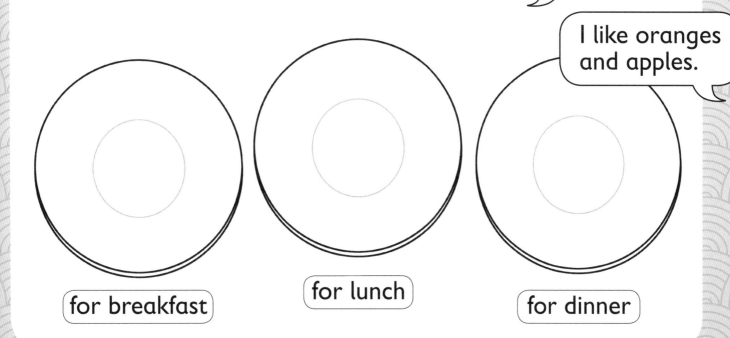

for breakfast

for lunch

for dinner

47

Grammar reference

1 Order the words.

1. Tom. | What's | his | He's | name?

_____ ? _____

2. Who's | She's | Mrs. | Brown. | my | teacher, | she?

_____ ? _____

2 Look and write.

Yes, there is.   Yes, there are.   No, there aren't.

1. Is there a whiteboard on the wall? ✓ _____
2. Are there three computers in the classroom? ✗ _____
3. Are there a lot of chairs in the classroom? ✓ _____

3 Circle the question and the answer.

Whoserobotisthis?It'sRobert's.

4 Match the questions and answers.

1. Whose red dress is that?   Yes, they are.
2. Whose blue pants are those?   It's mine.
3. Are those blue boots yours?   They're Dad's.

5 Look and complete.

'm not	'm	're	're not	's	's not

(1) ✓ I _____ singing.

(2) ✗ I _____ dancing.

(3) ✓ You _____ reading.

(4) ✗ He _____ running.

(5) ✓ She _____ playing tennis.

(6) ✗ We _____ painting.

6 Circle the question and the answer.

CanIhavesomefish,please?Hereyouare.

7 Look and write.

So do I.   I don't.   So do I.

(1) I like rabbits.   ☺ _____

(2) I like donkeys.   ☺ _____

(3) I like spiders.   ☹ _____

8 Look and complete.

(1) Where's the café?   It's **bhnide** _____ the school.

(2) Where's the park?   It's **ni ofrnt fo** _____ the hospital.

(3) Where's the store?   It's **teewenb** _____ the park and the apartments.

Thanks and Acknowledgments

Authors' thanks

Many thanks to everyone at Cambridge University Press and in particular to:

Rosemary Bradley for supervising the whole project and for her keen editorial eye;
Emily Hird for her energy, enthusiasm, and enormous organisational capacity;
Colin Sage for his good ideas and helpful suggestions;
Claire Appleyard for her editorial contribution.

Many thanks to Karen Elliot for her expertise and enthusiasm in the writing of the Phonics sections.

We would also like to thank all our pupils and colleagues at Star English, El Palmar, Murcia, and especially Jim Kelly and Julie Woodman for their help and suggestions at various stages of the project.

Dedications

I would like to dedicate this book to the women who have been my pillars of strength: Milagros Marín, Sara de Alba, Elia Navarro, and Maricarmen Balsalobre - CN

To Paloma, for her love, encouragement, and unwavering support. Thanks. - MT

The Authors and Publishers would like to thank the following teachers for their help in reviewing the material and for the invaluable feedback they provided:

Alice Matovich, Cecilia Sanchez, Florencia Durante, Maria Loe Antigona, Argentina; Erica Santos, Brazil; Ma Xin, Ren Xiaochi, China; Albeiro Monsalve Marin, Colombia; Agata Jankiewicz, Poland; Maria Antonia Castro, Spain; Catherine Taylor, Turkey.

The authors and publishers would like to thank the following consultants for their invaluable feedback:

Coralyn Bradshaw, Pippa Mayfield, Hilary Ratcliff, Melanie Williams.

We would also like to thank all the teachers who allowed us to observe their classes and who gave up their invaluable time for interviews and focus groups.

The authors and publishers are grateful to the following illustrators:

Andrew Hennessey; Beatrice Costamagna, c/o Pickled ink; Chris Garbutt, c/o Arena; Emily Skinner, c/o Graham-Cameron Illustration; Gary Swift; James Elston, c/o Syvlie Poggio; Kelly Kennedy, c/o Syvlie Poggio; Lisa Smith; Lisa Williams, c/o Syvlie Poggio; Marie Simpson, c/o Pickled ink; Matt Ward, c/o Beehive; Melanie Sharp, c/o Syvlie Poggio.

The authors and publishers acknowledge the following sources of copyright material and are grateful for the permissions granted. While every effort has been made, it has not always been possible to identify the sources of all the material used or to trace all copyright holders. If any omissions are brought to our notice, we will be happy to include the appropriate acknowledgments on reprinting.

p.17 (background): Thinkstock; p.31 (background): Thinkstock; p.45 (background): Thinkstock.

The publishers are grateful to the following contributors:

Louise Edgeworth: picture research and art direction
Wild Apple Design Ltd: page design
Blooberry: additional design
John Green and Tim Woolf, TEFL Audio: audio recordings
John Marshall Media, Inc. and Lisa Hutchins: audio recordings for the American English edition
Robert Lee: song writing
hyphen S.A.: publishing management, American English edition

Hi again! (page 9)

 **black**  purple  yellow

 green  pink  blue

 Back to school (page 15)

 Play time! (page 23)

  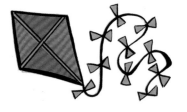

4 At home (page 29)

 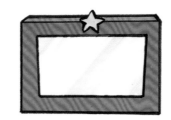 

5 Meet my family (page 39)

6 Dinner time (page 45)